PIRANHAS

by Mary Berendes

Published in the United States of America by The Child's World®
1980 Lookout Drive • Mankato, MN 56003-1705
800-599-READ • www.childsworld.com

PHOTO CREDITS

© Chris Catton/Survival/OSF/Animals Animals–Earth Scenes: 22
© Claus Meyer/Minden Pictures: 8–9
© Ian Beames/ardea.com: 17
© iStockphoto.com/Kristen Johansen: 3, 31
© John Madere/Corbis: 14–15
© Johnny Jensen/imagequestmarine.com: 10–11, 13
© Manor Photography/Alamy: 4–5
© Paul A. Zahl/Getty Images: 21
© Redmond Durrell/Alamy: 7
© R. Jackman/OSF/Animals Animals–Earth Scenes: 27
© Tierbild Okapia/Hans Reinhard/Photo Researchers, Inc.: 28–29
© Tom Brakefield/Corbis: cover, 1
© Tom McHugh/Photo Researchers, Inc.: 18
© W. Perry Conway/Corbis: 24–25

ACKNOWLEDGMENTS

The Child's World®: Mary Berendes, Publishing Director;
Katherine Stevenson, Editor; Pamela Mitsakos, Photo Researcher;
Judy Karren, Fact Checker

The Design Lab: Kathleen Petelinsek, Design; Kari Tobin, Page Production

LIBRARY OF CONGRESS CATALOGING-IN-PUBLICATION DATA

Berendes, Mary.
  Piranhas / by Mary Berendes.
     p. cm. — (New naturebooks)
  Includes index.
  ISBN-13: 978-1-59296-851-0 (library bound : alk. paper)
  ISBN-10: 1-59296-851-1 (library bound : alk. paper)
  1. Piranhas—Juvenile literature. I. Title. II. Series.
  QL638.C5B47 2007
  597'.48—dc22   2007000180

Table of Contents

On the cover: You can clearly see this red-bellied piranha's sharp teeth.

Meet the Piranha!

"Piranha" means "toothed fish."

"Piranha" can be pronounced either puh-RAH-nuh or puh-RAHN-yah.

A river flows slowly through the South American jungle. Under the water's surface, animals of all kinds swim and live. Near the shore, colorful fish are splashing and jumping in a large group. They are biting away pieces of meat from a dead catfish. What could these hungry fish be? They're piranhas!

These red-bellied piranhas are watching for their next meal. Red-bellies are also called Natterer's piranhas.

What Do Piranhas Look Like?

It's hard to tell the difference between male and female piranhas just by looking at them.

Piranhas keep replacing their teeth throughout their lives, so the teeth are always very sharp.

Piranhas are beautiful fish. Many are brightly colored with red, green, or black markings. They have round, flat bodies and stubby snouts. But piranhas are best known for their teeth. The teeth are triangular, strong, and razor sharp. The piranha's lower jaw sticks out farther than its upper jaw. The teeth close together like a trap. Once a piranha bites something, it can tear at it easily.

This red-bellied piranha is showing its sharp teeth as it swims just below the surface.

Where Do Piranhas Live?

Piranhas don't live in South America's mountain lakes or streams. The water is too cold.

Piranhas are freshwater **tropical** fish. They come from rivers, lakes, and streams in several parts of South America. They live in places where the water is warm all year long. Some of the most famous rivers with piranhas are the Amazon, the Orinoco, and the La Plata.

Sometimes piranhas appear in other parts of the world where they don't belong. They have been found in North America and even as far away as the Ukraine. They got to these places because people kept them as pets and then turned them loose. If conditions are right, **invasive** animals such as these can live and grow, causing damage to other plants and animals.

Piraya piranhas like this one are also called black-tailed piranhas. They live in Brazil.

8

Are There Different Kinds of Piranhas?

Some scientists think piranhas swim in groups to protect themselves from enemies.

Some piranhas can grow to nearly 24 inches (61 cm) long.

There are about 25 different kinds, or **species**, of piranhas. The most common is the red-bellied piranha. Its name comes from the bright red color on its underside. Red-bellied piranhas can grow up to 16 inches (41 cm) long. They often have gold or silver backs with darker tails.

Another type of piranha is the black piranha. It has red eyes and very strong jaws. An adult black piranha's jaws are so strong, it can bite through a piece of wood!

You can see the red eye and sturdy jaws of this black piranha.

10

What Are Baby Piranhas Like?

When piranhas build nests, they clear an area by moving stones and chewing up plants.

Both piranha parents guard their eggs.

A piranha defending its eggs might be more likely to bite or attack.

Little is known about how piranhas have their young. Most scientists agree that piranhas mate during the rainy season, when the water is deeper. They also think that adult females lay eggs on floating water plants or in nests made in the mud. When the eggs hatch, tiny piranhas swim out and hide in nearby plants and rocks. When they are big enough, the young piranhas swim out in the open and join the adults.

This baby red-bellied piranha lives in an aquarium. You can see some adult red-bellies on page 5.

12

What Do Piranhas Eat?

Piranhas rarely attack healthy prey. Instead, they prefer to eat dead or dying animals.

Piranha babies might eat each other if they are hungry and there is little other food.

Piranhas eat almost anything. Some eat seeds or fruits that fall into the water. Others wait for insects or smaller fish to swim by. Some piranhas eat the tails and fins of larger fish. A few kinds even bite the toes of animals that walk or swim through the water. Most piranhas are also **scavengers** that eat dead animals. By eating dead creatures, piranhas keep rivers and lakes clean.

These piranhas live in a zoo. They are being fed live goldfish to eat.

14

How Do Piranhas Eat?

Piranhas can tell when there's a single drop of blood in 50 gallons (189 liters) of water.

An animal splashing and making noise in the water can cause a piranha feeding frenzy.

Piranhas like blood. In fact, they can even smell it! When an animal is bleeding in the water, a few piranhas will swim toward it. If they can, they bite little pieces from the animal. That makes the animal bleed some more. As more piranhas smell the blood, they swim toward the animal. Soon, the water is full of hungry, biting piranhas. This is called a **feeding frenzy**.

These hungry piranhas live at another zoo. They are searching for the food that was just placed in their tank.

When piranhas eat, they use their teeth only to cut and bite. They never chew their food. Instead, they swallow it whole. That way, they can eat very quickly. With so many piranhas eating during a feeding frenzy, the food disappears fast. Each piranha eats quickly to get all the food it can!

Piranhas' taste buds cover their bodies. That helps the fish decide whether things floating or swimming by would be good to eat.

Piranhas might go for days without food and stuff themselves when they get the chance.

Piranhas often swim together in groups like this one.

Are Piranhas Dangerous?

People in South America often swim in water where there are piranhas. But they are careful. It's not a good idea to go swimming near piranhas if you have an open cut!

Piranhas usually leave people and larger animals alone. But during certain times of the year, they attack more often. When the weather is very dry, the piranhas' rivers and lakes begin to dry up. When this happens, the piranhas have less room and less food. They begin to attack everything in the water—even each other! During the dry season, injured or weak animals can be eaten quickly if they enter waters where hungry piranhas live.

20

These red-bellied piranhas are swimming in shallow water during Brazil's dry season.

The most dangerous piranhas, though, are the ones in a feeding frenzy. They are very excited and will snap and bite at almost anything. If you put your hand in the water during a feeding frenzy, the piranhas would probably bite you by mistake. That's why South Americans stay out of the water when piranhas are in a feeding frenzy. Otherwise, they would be food for the piranhas, too!

Pet piranhas can get excited when they eat, too! People who keep piranhas must feed them carefully.

Piranhas usually rest at night and are most active at dawn.

Piranhas in a feeding frenzy don't know—or care—what they are biting! They swim over and around each other. They dart around and splash near the surface.

23

Do Piranhas Have Any Enemies?

If a piranha gets caught on a hook and line, other piranhas might attack it.

People who fish for piranhas must handle them carefully when they take them out of the water. Otherwise they might get bitten.

Even though piranhas can be dangerous, many other animals like to eat them. Wading birds and fish eat young and small piranhas. Larger piranhas are often eaten by crocodiles called *caimans*. Many people like to eat piranhas, too. South Americans use everything from strings to nets to catch these delicious fish.

This hungry caiman has caught a red-bellied piranha to eat.

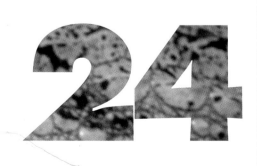

Are Piranhas Important?

Piranhas are very important. They keep rivers and lakes clean by eating dead fish and other animals. Fruit-eating piranhas help, too. By carrying fruit seeds in their waste, they spread different kinds of plants throughout the rivers and lakes.

Scary movies and stories show piranhas as mean, angry fish that like to attack people and animals. But that isn't really true. They might be dangerous, but they don't bite to be mean. They bite when they are hungry, scared, or excited.

How do you think berry-eating piranhas like this one got their name?

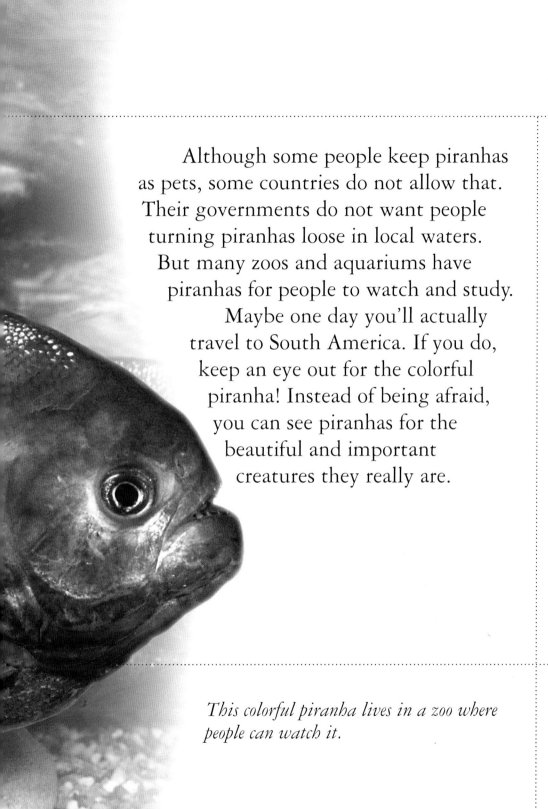

Although some people keep piranhas as pets, some countries do not allow that. Their governments do not want people turning piranhas loose in local waters. But many zoos and aquariums have piranhas for people to watch and study. Maybe one day you'll actually travel to South America. If you do, keep an eye out for the colorful piranha! Instead of being afraid, you can see piranhas for the beautiful and important creatures they really are.

This colorful piranha lives in a zoo where people can watch it.

Piranhas can live to be about eight years old.

People in South America use piranha teeth as cutting tools.

29

Glossary

feeding frenzy (FEE-ding FREN-zee) When animals are in a feeding frenzy, they eat quickly, in a wild and excited way. Piranhas sometimes go into feeding frenzies.

invasive (in-VAY-siv) Invasive species are ones people bring to lands where they don't belong and where they can do harm. Releasing pet fish such as piranhas can turn them into invasive species.

prey (PRAY) Prey are animals that other animals hunt as food. Piranhas don't usually attack healthy prey.

scavengers (SKAV-un-jerz) Animals that are scavengers will feed on whatever garbage they find, including dead animals. Piranhas are scavengers.

species (SPEE-sheez) An animal species is a group of animals that share the same features and can have babies only with animals in the same group. There are about 25 species of piranha.

tropical (TRAH-pih-kull) Tropical areas are those that have warm, moist weather all year long. Piranhas are tropical fish.

To Find Out More

Read It!

Dollar, Sam. *Piranhas.* Austin, TX: Steadwell Books, 2001.

Landau, Elaine. *Piranhas.* New York: Children's Press, 1999.

Lynett, Rachel. *Piranha.* San Diego, CA: Kidhaven Press, 2004.

Schulte, Mary. *Piranhas and Other Fish.* New York: Children's Press, 2005.

On the Web

Visit our Web page for lots of links about piranhas:
http://www.childsworld.com/links

Note to Parents, Teachers, and Librarians: We routinely check our
Web links to make sure they're safe, active sites—so encourage
your readers to check them out!

31

Index

About the Author

Mary Berendes has loved books and writing for as long as she can remember. An author of over twenty children's books, Mary especially enjoys writing about nature and animals. Mary has long been a collector of antique books, and owns several that are more than two hundred years old. She lives in Minnesota.